Easy Sweets
No-Bake Desserts to Satisfy Your Sweet Tooth Without Touching the Oven

Copyright © 2021

All rights reserved.

DEDICATION

The author and publisher have provided this e-book to you for your personal use only. You may not make this e-book publicly available in any way. Copyright infringement is against the law. If you believe the copy of this e-book you are reading infringes on the author's copyright, please notify the publisher at: https://us.macmillan.com/piracy

Contents

No-Bake Cheesecake with Berry Toppings 1

Raspberry and Pistachio Semifreddo 5

Chamomile-Mascarpone Tart With Fresh Strawberries .. 8

Hot Fudge Golden Grahams Parfait 12

Lemon Creme Sandwich Cookies 15

Pickled Gingery Plums 18

Vanilla Yogurt and Berry Trifle 20

Golden Oreo Truffles 24

Lemon Cream Pie 35

Fruity Pebble Rice Krispies Treats 40

Raspberry Cheesecake Bars 46

Mini Key Lime Pies 55

Buckeye Peanut Butter Balls 59

Chocolate Lasagna 63

No-Bake Chocolate Oatmeal Bars 73

Easy Sweets

No-Bake Cheesecake with Berry Toppings

Customize this beautiful cheesecake with your favorite fruit. Not only is it bursting with flavor, but it also takes just 30 minutes to prep.

Easy Sweets

The only thing better than the way this elegant cheesecake looks is how simple it is to put together—there's no baking required.

YIELDS:

10 servings

PREP TIME:

0 hours 30 mins

TOTAL TIME:

6 hours 30 mins

INGREDIENTS

Cheesecake

25 vanilla wafers

3/4 c. roasted, salted almonds

4 tbsp. (1/2 stick) unsalted butter, melted

1/2 c. plus 2 tablespoons granulated sugar, divided

1 3/4 c. cold heavy cream

Easy Sweets

1 (0.25-oz.) envelope unflavored gelatin

1 1/2 c. plain Greek yogurt

1 (8-ounce) package cream cheese, at room temperature

2 tsp. pure vanilla extract

1/4 tsp. Kosher salt

Raspberry Topping

2 tbsp. granulated sugar

1 tbsp. light rum

2 tsp. lime zest

2 c. fresh raspberries

Blackberry Topping

2 tbsp. light brown sugar

2 tbsp. Chopped fresh mint

1 tbsp. bourbon

1/4 tsp. pure vanilla extract

Easy Sweets

2 c. lightly mashed fresh blackberries

Blueberry Topping

2 tbsp. granulated sugar

2 tsp. lemon zest

1 tbsp. lemon juice

2 c. fresh blueberries

Strawberry Topping

2 tbsp. granulated sugar

2 tbsp. chopped fresh basil

1 tsp. balsamic vinegar

2 c. sliced fresh strawberries

DIRECTIONS

Pulse wafers and almonds in a food processor until finely ground, 12 to 14 times. Add butter and 2 tablespoons sugar; pulse until well combined. Press mixture into bottom of a 9-inch springform pan. Freeze 20 minutes or up to 1 day.

Easy Sweets

Pour cream in a medium saucepan; sprinkle gelatin over top. Let stand 10 minutes. Cook cream mixture over medium-low heat, stirring constantly, until gelatin is dissolved, 4 to 6 minutes. Cool 10 minutes.

In a clean food processor, process yogurt, cream cheese, vanilla, salt, and remaining 1/2 cup sugar until smooth, about 1 minute. Add cream mixture and process until well combined.

Pour filling into crust and smooth with a rubber spatula. Cover pan with plastic wrap and chill until firm, at least 6 hours or up to 2 days.

To make the berry toppings, toss together each respective topping's ingredients and then the berries; let macerate, stirring occasionally, until mixture is syrupy, about 20 minutes.

When cake pan is ready, run a knife around sides of pan and remove ring. Serve with desired berry toppings.

Raspberry and Pistachio Semifreddo

This sweet semi-frozen custardy dessert makes the most of fresh berries and works just as well with blackberries or blueberries.

Easy Sweets

Use a long serrated knife to cut clean slices. In place of the raspberries, substitute an equal amount of blueberries or chopped

Easy Sweets

strawberries.

YIELDS:

6 servings

TOTAL TIME:

4 hours 40 mins

INGREDIENTS

1/4 c. cold sour cream

1/2 c. confectioners' sugar

1 c. cold heavy cream

1/4 c. pistachios, chopped

2 pt. raspberries, divided

1 tbsp. fresh lemon juice

1 tbsp. pure honey

2 tbsp. fresh mint leaves

DIRECTIONS

Line an 8-by-4-inch loaf pan with plastic wrap, leaving an overhang on all four sides.

Beat sour cream with an electric mixer on medium speed until smooth, 1 minute. Add sugar and beat to combine. Reduce mixer speed to low and gradually beat in heavy cream. Increase speed to medium and beat until stiff peaks form, 2 to 3 minutes.

Fold in pistachios and 1 pint raspberries; transfer to prepared pan. Freeze until set, at least 4 hours or up to 1 week.

Whisk together lemon juice and honey in a bowl until dissolved. Add remaining raspberries and toss to combine. Let sit, tossing occasionally, 18 to 20 minutes. Invert semifreddo onto a platter; discard plastic. Top with raspberries and mint leaves.

Chamomile-Mascarpone Tart With Fresh Strawberries

The smart addition of chamomile turns a traditional tart into a surprisingly complex dessert. Use a no-bake pie crust, and you'll never have to turn on the oven.

Easy Sweets

Chamomile tea adds an unexpectedly fruity layer to this sweet

Easy Sweets

seasonal treat.

YIELDS:

8 servings

TOTAL TIME:

1 hour 30 mins

INGREDIENTS

3/4 c. heavy cream

1/4 c. plus 1 tablespoon loose chamomile tea, divided

3/4 c. (1 1/2 sticks) unsalted butter, at room temperature

1/3 c. confectioners' sugar

1 tsp. vanilla bean paste

Pinch of kosher salt

2 c. all-purpose flour, spooned and leveled

2 tbsp. granulated sugar

3/4 c. mascarpone

Easy Sweets

1 lb. strawberries, sliced

Fresh chamomile flowers, for serving

DIRECTIONS

Bring cream to a simmer in a small saucepan. Add 1/4 cup tea and let steep for 5 minutes. Strain through a wire-mesh strainer lined with cheesecloth; discard tea. Refrigerate until cold.

Preheat oven to 400°F. Beat butter, confectioners' sugar, vanilla, and salt with an electric mixer on medium speed until light and fluffy, 1 to 3 minutes. Reduce mixer speed to low and beat in flour just until combined. Shape dough into a ball, then transfer to a work surface and roll between two pieces of parchment paper to 1/8 inch thick. Fit on bottom and up the sides of a 9-inch removable- bottom tart pan. (Cut away any overhanging dough by gently running a rolling pin over the rim of the pan.) Place on a baking sheet, poke bottoms and sides with a fork and refrigerate until firm, 15 to 20 minutes. Bake until golden brown, 14 to 16 minutes. Let cool completely.

Meanwhile, grind granulated sugar and remaining tablespoon tea in a spice grinder until finely chopped, 15 to 30 seconds. Whisk together mascarpone, chamomile cream, and chamomile sugar with an electric mixer on medium-high speed until stiff peaks form, 1 to 2 minutes. Spread into crust. Top with strawberries and flowers.

Hot Fudge Golden Grahams Parfait

Kids will love to make their own ice cream sundaes. It's an easy and classic treat to cool down on a hot summer day.

Easy Sweets

This sweet cereal is the ultimate ice cream sundae topping.

YIELDS:

8 servings

TOTAL TIME:

1 hour 30 mins

INGREDIENTS

Ice Cream Parfait

Cooking spray

1 c. sugar

3 tbsp. pure honey

3/4 tsp. Kosher salt

1/4 tsp. baking soda

2 1/2 c. Golden Grahams Cereal

1/2 c. Toasted sliced almonds

2 pints vanilla ice cream

Easy Sweets

Whipped cream and cherries, for garnish

Spicy Hot Fudge Sauce

1/2 c. cocoa powder

1/3 c. packed light brown sugar

1/2 c. heavy cream

2 tbsp. corn syrup

4 tbsp. unsalted butter

1 1/2 tsp. pure vanilla extract

1/2 tsp. ground cinnamon

Pinch of cayenne

DIRECTIONS

Line a rimmed baking sheet with parchment paper; lightly grease. Bring sugar, honey, and 3 tablespoons water to a boil in a medium saucepan over medium heat. Cook, without stirring, until mixture is a deep-amber color, 6 to 7 minutes; remove from heat. Immediately stir in salt and baking soda, then quickly stir in cereal and almonds.

Easy Sweets

Spread mixture, with a rubber spatula, in an even layer on prepared baking sheet. Let cool until hardened, 40 to 45 minutes. Break into clusters.

Make Spicy Hot Fudge Sauce: Whisk together cocoa powder and light brown sugar in a medium saucepan. Whisk in heavy cream and corn syrup. Cook over medium heat until warm, 4 to 5 minutes. Remove from heat and stir in unsalted butter, pure vanilla extract, ground cinnamon, and cayenne until smooth. Cool, whisking occasionally, until just warm, 15 to 20 minutes.

Layer Spicy Hot Fudge Sauce, brittle, and scoops of ice cream in parfait glasses. Garnish with whipped cream and cherries.

Lemon Creme Sandwich Cookies

Turn store-bought cookies into a flavor-packed dessert with fast made-from-scratch lemon frosting.

Easy Sweets

Easy Sweets

These easy lemon cookies are half-homemade, half store-bought, and totally delicious.

YIELDS:

32 servings

INGREDIENTS

2 oz. softened cream cheese

3 tbsp. confectioners' sugar

1/2 tsp. lemon zest

2 tbsp. lemon juice

1/2 c. heavy cream

32 thin lemon cookies

DIRECTIONS

Beat softened cream cheese with an electric mixer on medium speed until smooth. Beat in confectioners' sugar, lemon zest, and lemon juice.

Slowly add cold heavy cream, beating until stiff peaks form.

Easy Sweets

Sandwich cream between 32 thin lemon cookies (about 2 teaspoon per sandwich). Makes 32 cookies.

Pickled Gingery Plums

There's nothing more refreshing on a hot summer's day than chilled fruit served over a scoop of ice cream.

Easy Sweets

Pickle plums and oranges with a sugary-sweet brine for a refreshing summer dessert.

Note: The total time does not include chilling time. We recommend chilling the pickled fruit for at least 1 day.

YIELDS:

8 servings

TOTAL TIME:

0 hours 15 mins

INGREDIENTS

1/2 c. unseasoned rice vinegar

1/2 c. pure honey

1/2 c. sugar

4 plums, cut into 6 wedges each

1/2 orange, cut into 6 wedges, then each wedge halved

1 2-inch piece fresh ginger, thinly sliced

Easy Sweets

8 sprigs thyme

1 vanilla bean, split

Vanilla ice cream, for serving

DIRECTIONS

Bring vinegar, honey, sugar, and 3/4 cup water to a boil in a small saucepan. Reduce heat and simmer until honey and sugar are dissolved.

Place plums, orange, ginger, thyme, and vanilla bean in a bowl or jar. Cover with brine; cool to room temperature. Chill at least 1 day and up to 3 days.

Serve plums over vanilla ice cream.

Vanilla Yogurt and Berry Trifle

This smartly impressive dessert keeps things light with Greek yogurt (although whipped cream works very well) and fresh berries. You can assemble it ahead of time, and keep it chilled until you're ready to serve.

Easy Sweets

Easy Sweets

CAL/SERV:

401

YIELDS:

10

PREP TIME:

0 hours 20 mins

TOTAL TIME:

0 hours 35 mins

INGREDIENTS

2 package frozen strawberries

1 package frozen raspberries

1 c. confectioners' sugar

1 1/2 tsp. cornstarch

3/4 c. heavy cream

3 container nonfat vanilla Greek yogurt

Easy Sweets

40 ladyfingers

2 tbsp. orange liqueur (optional)

1 package frozen blueberries

DIRECTIONS

In a medium saucepan over medium heat, whisk together raspberry and strawberry juices with 2/3 cup sugar and cornstarch. Boil until thickened, 1 to 2 minutes. Transfer to a medium bowl and refrigerate until cool, about 20 minutes.

Meanwhile, in a medium bowl, whip heavy cream to stiff peaks; set aside. In a large bowl, combine yogurt and remaining 2/3 cup sugar. Fold in whipped cream.

Break ladyfingers in half. Place half of them in a 2-quart glass bowl or trifle dish. Drizzle cookies with 1 tablespoon liqueur, if using, and dollop with one-third of yogurt mixture. Spoon half of berries over yogurt mixture, then drizzle 3 to 4 tablespoons thickened juices. Layer another one-third of yogurt mixture over berries, followed by a layer of remaining ladyfingers. Drizzle with remaining 1 tablespoon liqueur and dollop with remaining yogurt mixture. Top with remaining berries and 3 to 4 more tablespoons thickened juice. Refrigerate until chilled, about 2 hours, before serving.

Tips & Techniques

Tip: A creamy filling made with nonfat yogurt saves you 211 calories and 16 grams of fat per serving, when compared with traditional custard.

Golden Oreo Truffles

Kids will have a blast dipping and dunking these bites, but they'll love decorating with rainbow sprinkles the most.

Easy Sweets

Ingredients

1 14.3 oz. package Golden Oreos

1 8 oz. block of cream cheese, softened

1 tsp vanilla extract

Easy Sweets

12 oz. white melting chocolate

sprinkles

HOW TO MAKE THESE OREO TRUFFLES:

Place cookies into a food processor and process until broken down into small crumbs. It is ok if you still have a few chunks here and there but for the most part, you want them ground up. If you don't

Easy Sweets

have a food processor, you can put them in a large plastic bag and crush them with a rolling pin. (steps 1 and 2)

Transfer Oreo cookie crumbs to a medium mixing bowl. Add in softened cream cheese and vanilla. As you can see, my cream cheese was very soft. Put it in the microwave for about 15 seconds or so to get it that way for easier mixing. I also scoop it onto the cookies in spoonfuls to break it up a bit. This also helps with mixing. (steps 3 and 4)

Easy Sweets

Easy Sweets

Mix cookie crumbs, cream cheese and vanilla until cream cheese is fully incorporated. You can use a spoon, or you can get your hands good and clean and knead the mixture to get everything combined. This is what I do most often. Perhaps a pair of gloves will help too!

Easy Sweets

(step 5)

Roll the mixture into bite sized balls. I manage to get 24 of these most of the time. The size of my truffle balls are about an inch and half in diameter. You can make yours smaller if that seems to big, but you may need more white chocolate to coat in the end. (step 6)

It is advised freezing the balls for at least 15 minutes here is possible. Sometimes I pop them in the freezer overnight even so they are super hard when it's time to coat them. (step 6)

When you are ready to coat your truffles, melt the white chocolate chips in the way you prefer. You can use a double boiler method or microwave them in 25 second increments. Stir in between and make sure you do NOT over heat the chocolate. (steps 7 and 8)

Easy Sweets

Coat the Oreo Truffles. I use two forks and dip a truffle into the melted chocolate. Using the two forks, roll the ball around, and then let excess chocolate drip off before placing on parchment paper or another surface. Use one of the forks to help push it nicely onto the

Easy Sweets

surface. (steps 9, 10 and 11)

You may want to have several forks to switch out here as well.

Add some sprinkles on top and allow chocolate to dry before serving. (step 12)

Store in the refrigerator for up to a week.

Easy Sweets

Easy Sweets

Easy Sweets

Lemon Cream Pie

Not only is this pie luscious, but it's also stunning. It could even be a centerpiece on your spring tablescape.

Prep time: 25 mins

Easy Sweets

Total time: 25 mins

NO BAKE LEMON CREAM PIE – Sweet, tart and incredibly easy pie, full of lemon flavor! This is definitely a refreshing, super delicious creamy dessert!

INGREDIENTS

For Graham Cracker Crusts:

1 ½ cups graham cracker crumbs

6 tablespoons unsalted butter, melted

¼ cup of sugar

For Lemon Cream Filling:

2 cups sweetened condensed milk

8 oz Mascarpone cheese

½ cup powdered sugar

1 cup heavy whipping cream

½ cup fresh lemon juice

Easy Sweets

For Topping:

1 cup heavy whipping cream

½ cup powdered sugar

Fresh lemon slices, optional

Easy Sweets

No Bake Lemon Cream Pie

INSTRUCTIONS

Spray 8 inch pie plate with non-stick spray, set aside

To make crust:

Easy Sweets

In a medium bowl, combine crushed graham crackers, butter and sugar and stir

Press mixture into bottom and up the sides of pie plate, press hard to compact (you can use a glass to press the bottom, but use your fingers to press the sides)

Place in the freezer while you make filling

To make lemon cream filling:

In a medium bowl, mix Mascarpone cheese and sugar until smooth and creamy, set aside

In separate bowl whip heavy cream until soft peaks form add lemon juice and continue mixing until stiff peaks form

Add Mascarpone cheese mixture into beaten heavy cream and mix on low speed just to combine

Slowly add condensed milk and beat until well mixed

Pour lemon cream mixture into prepared pie plate and refrigerate for at least 6 hours or until firm

To make topping:

Beat heavy cream and powdered sugar together in a mixer until stiff peaks form

Spread or pipe the whipped cream on top of the cooled pie, add some lemon slices, if desired

Serve

Fruity Pebble Rice Krispies Treats

Upgrade your classic Rice Krispies Treats recipe by switching out the typical rice cereal for Fruity Pebbles. They're an unexpected—and fun—swap.

Easy Sweets

Colorful, sweet, and easy-to-make Fruity Pebbles Rice Krispies Treats

Easy Sweets

will be a hit wherever you serve them! These treats take minutes to assemble, are easy to transport, and require only six ingredients.

prep time

10 minutes

setting up time

10 minutes

total time

10 minutes

servings

12 bars

calories

586kcal

INGREDIENTS

5 tablespoons (71g) unsalted butter

10 ounces mini marshmallows, (one bag), divided

Easy Sweets

1/4 teaspoon fine sea salt (if using table salt, use 1/8 teaspoon)

1 teaspoon pure vanilla extract

2 cups (58g) plain Rice Krispies cereal (See Note 1)

4 cups (217g) Fruity Pebbles cereal

INSTRUCTIONS

Line a 9×9-inch pan with parchment paper with an overhang for easy removal. Spray parchment paper with cooking spray. Set aside.

In a large nonstick pan, melt the butter over low heat. Once the butter is completely melted, add in all but 2 and 1/2 cups (120g) of the marshmallows. Stir constantly, keeping the heat on low, until the marshmallows are completely melted.

As soon as the marshmallows are just melted, remove the pan from the heat. Stir in the salt and vanilla extract. Next, stir in the Rice Krispies and Fruity Pebbles cereals very gently. Stir in the reserved 2 and 1/2 cups marshmallows. Stir until combined.

Pour the mixture into the lined and prepared pan. Lightly spritz your hands with cooking spray and gently (do not press hard/compact or

Easy Sweets

you'll get hard bars) press the bars evenly into the pan.

Allow the bars to cool and set up before using the overhang to pull the bars out and cut them into squares. Bars are best enjoyed the same day.

RECIPE NOTES

Note 1: You can use all fruity pebbles instead of the Rice Krispies/Pebbles mix, but I found it to be a little too sweet. Plain Rice Krispies aren't highly sweetened, while Fruity Pebbles are.

Easy Sweets

Raspberry Cheesecake Bars

A buttery graham cracker crust, smooth cheesecake filling, and sweet raspberry swirl means every bite of these bars is bursting with different flavors and textures. As soon as you finish your first bar, you'll be reaching for another—and another!

Easy Sweets

Prep Time: 10 minutes

Resting Time: 1 hour 10 minutes

Total Time: 1 hour 20 minutes

Servings: 16 bars

INGREDIENTS

GRAHAM CRACKER CRUST

9 (157 g) graham cracker sheets

1/4 cup (32 g) confectioners' sugar

1/2 cup (113 g or 1 stick) unsalted butter, room temperature

1/2 teaspoon kosher salt

RASPBERRY PURÉE

1/2 cup (60 g) fresh raspberries

2 tablespoons granulated sugar

CHEESECAKE FILLING

16 ounces (170 g) cream cheese, room temperature

Easy Sweets

1 cup (125 g) confectioners' sugar

2 tablespoons fresh lemon juice

1 tablespoon lemon zest

1/2 teaspoon vanilla extract

1/2 teaspoon kosher salt

Easy Sweets

INSTRUCTIONS

GRAHAM CRACKER CRUST

Line an 8×8 baking pan with parchment paper and set aside. In a plastic bag, crush the graham crackers finely with the bottom of a measuring cup. In a large bowl, combine graham crackers, 1/4 cup confectioners' sugar, salt, and melted butter. Stir the mixture the mixture is the texture resembles wet sand. Dump the graham cracker mixture into the prepared pan. Press the mixture down with your hands to create an even layer. Freeze for 10 minutes.

RASPBERRY PURÉE

Place raspberries in the bowl of a food processor and sprinkle sugar on top. Let the berries sit for 15 minutes so the raspberries get juicy. Pulse the berries until smooth, about ten 1-second pulses. Press through a fine mesh strainer, discarding any seeds and pulp that remain. Stir in the sugar. Set aside and make the cheesecake mixture.

CHEESECAKE FILLING

In a separate bowl, combine cream cheese, confectioner's sugar, lemon juice, lemon zest and vanilla, stirring until smooth. Spread the

Easy Sweets

cream cheese mixture evenly on top of the graham cracker crust.

Dollop spoonfuls of the raspberry purée on top of the unbaked cheesecake. Use a skewer or knife to make swirls.

Freeze cheesecake bars uncovered for one hour. Transfer the frozen cheesecake onto a cutting board, peeling away the parchment paper. With a sharp knife, cut into bars. Store in an airtight container in the fridge (or freezer) and serve cold.

NOTES

Store cheesecake bars in an airtight container in the fridge for 3 days or freezer for 2 weeks. Serve cold.

Easy Sweets

Easy Sweets

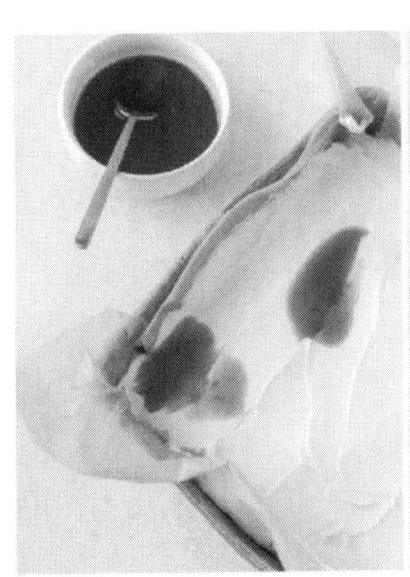

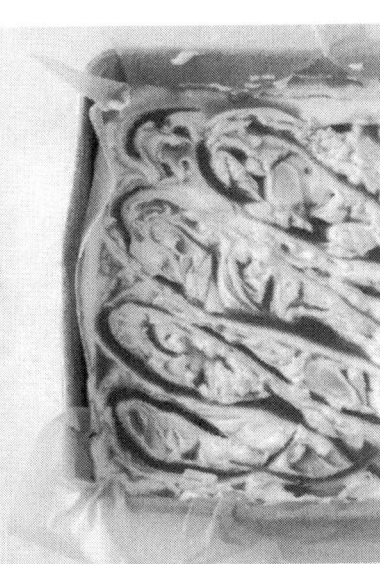

Easy Sweets

Easy Sweets

Easy Sweets

Mini Key Lime Pies
You can customize the crust with these fruit-filled bites

Easy Sweets

Ingredients

2 large eggs

2/3 cup granulated sugar

1/2 cup key lime juice

1/4 cup butter

1 package Keebler Ready Crust Mini Graham Cracker

1 cup Cool Whip

1 fresh key lime, cut into slices

6 raspberries

mint leaves

Instructions

Place a small saucepan with water on the stove and heat to a low boil.

Whisk together the eggs, sugar, and key lime juice in a glass bowl.

Place the bowl over the top of the simmering water. Make sure the bowl fits tightly, so the steam doesn't come out.

Easy Sweets

Stir the mixture constantly until it reaches 180 degrees and thickens.

Remove from the heat and stir in the butter until smooth.

Spoon the key lime curd evenly into the mini graham cracker crusts. Press a small piece of plastic wrap on top of each pie, directly on the surface. Refrigerate until chilled.

Remove the plastic wrap. Use a piping bag and icing tip 1M to swirl Cool Whip on top of each pie.

Top with a key lime slice, raspberry, and mint leaves right before serving.

YIELD: 6

SERVING SIZE: 1

Easy Sweets

Buckeye Peanut Butter Balls

It really doesn't get much simpler than these classic bites. They require just five ingredients and come together in 20 minutes.

Easy Sweets

PREP TIME

30 MINUTES

TOTAL TIME

30 MINUTES

SERVINGS

24 PEANUT BUTTER BALLS

INGREDIENTS

1 1/2 cups creamy peanut butter

1 cup butter

6 cups powdered sugar

1 teaspoon vanilla

4 cups semi-sweet chocolate chips

INSTRUCTIONS

Start by adding peanut butter, butter, vanilla and powdered sugar to a large bowl and mix until dough forms. Roll into 1 inch balls and put onto a waxed paper lined cookie sheet. Freeze until firm 20-30 minutes.

Easy Sweets

Melt chocolate chips in the microwave stirring every 30 seconds until smooth. Press a toothpick into the top of each ball and dip into the chocolate. Drizzle the tops with melted chocolate and sprinkle with sea salt if desired.

Easy Sweets

Chocolate Lasagna

Need to feed a crowd? This irresistible layered treat yields 16 servings.

Easy Sweets

This chocolate lasagna is a cookie crust topped with layers of cheesecake filling, pudding, whipped cream and chocolate chips. An impressive no bake dessert that's perfect for feeding a crowd!

Prep Time 40 minutes

Cook Time 1 minute

Chill Time 3 hours

Total Time 41 minutes

Servings

16

INGREDIENTS

For the crust

1 package Oreo cookies

6 tablespoons butter melted

cooking spray

For the cream cheese layer

Easy Sweets

8 ounces cream cheese softened

1/4 cup sugar

2 tablespoons milk or cream

1/2 teaspoon vanilla extract

1 1/2 cups whipped topping

For the pudding layer

2 3.9 ounce packages of chocolate pudding mix

3 1/4 cups milk

For the topping

1 bag miniature chocolate chips

3 cups whipped topping such as Cool Whip (thawed)

INSTRUCTIONS

For the crust

Coat a 9"x13" pan with cooking spray.

Easy Sweets

Place the Oreo cookies in a food processor and process until fine crumbs form.

Transfer the Oreo crumbs to a bowl and pour in the butter. Stir until thoroughly combined.

Firmly press the Oreo mixture into the bottom of the pan with your

Easy Sweets

fingers or the bottom of a measuring cup.

Freeze the pan for 10 minutes to set the crust.

For the cream cheese layer

Place the cream cheese in the bowl of a mixer. Beat until smooth and fluffy.

Add the sugar, milk and vanilla extract and beat until smooth.

Fold 1 1/2 cups of the whipped topping into the cream cheese mixture.

Easy Sweets

Spread the cream cheese mixture in an even layer over the Oreo crust.

Place the pan in the freezer for 10-15 minutes to chill.

For the pudding layer

Place the packages of chocolate pudding in a bowl and add 3 1/4 cups milk. Whisk until smooth and starting to thicken, 2-3 minutes.

Spread the pudding in an even layer over the cream cheese layer.

Place the pan in the freezer for 10-15 minutes to chill.

For the topping

Pipe or spread 3 cups whipped topping over the pudding layer. Sprinkle with chocolate chips.

Cover the pan loosely and chill in the refrigerator for a minimum of 3 hours or up to 3 days.

Cut into squares and serve. For the cleanest slices, place the pan in the freezer for 30 minutes prior to slicing.

Easy Sweets

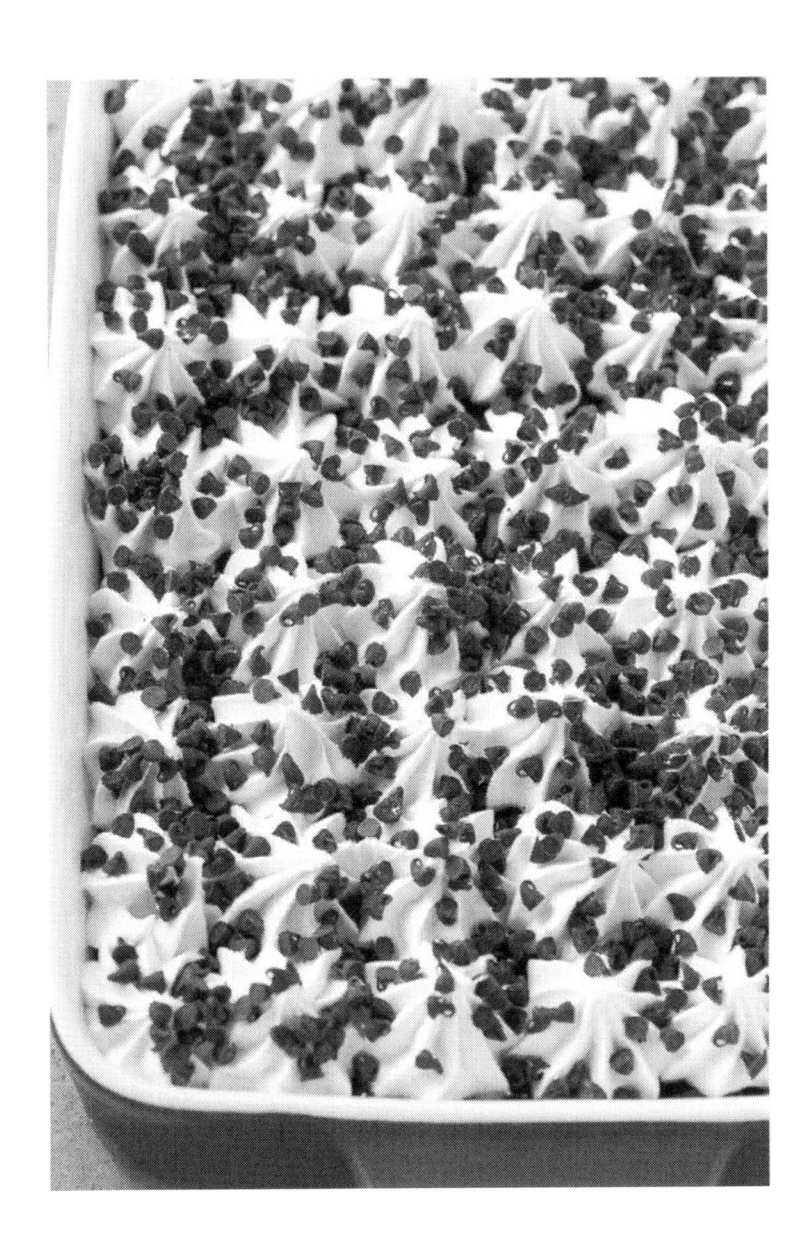

Easy Sweets

Easy Sweets

Easy Sweets

No-Bake Chocolate Oatmeal Bars

If it has oatmeal in its name, that means its fine for breakfast, right?! It will be hard to say no to these chocolatey peanut butter-filled bars.

Easy Sweets

PREP TIME

15 mins

CHILL TIME

2 hrs

TOTAL TIME

2 hrs 15 mins

SERVINGS

16 -20

INGREDIENTS

1 cup butter

1/2 cup brown sugar packed

1 teaspoon vanilla extract

3 cups rolled oats

1 cup semisweet or dark chocolate chips

1/2 cup peanut butter

Easy Sweets

INSTRUCTIONS

Line an 8-inch or 9-inch square baking dish with parchment paper and set aside. Overhangs the edges of the foil to lift the bars easier from the baking dish. (You can use a 9x13-inch if you want thinner bars.)

Melt butter and brown sugar in large saucepan over medium heat, until the butter has melted and the sugar has dissolved. Stir in vanilla. Mix in the oats.

Cook over low heat 3 to 4 minutes, or until ingredients are well blended.

Pour half of the oat mixture into the prepared baking dish. Spread out the mixture evenly, pressing down. Reserve the other half for second layer.

To make the filling, melt the peanut butter and chocolate chips together in a small microwave-safe bowl and stir until it's smooth.

Pour the chocolate mixture over the crust in the pan, reserving about 1/4 cup for drizzling and spread evenly.

Easy Sweets

Pour the remaining oat mixture over the chocolate layer, pressing in gently and drizzle with the remaining chocolate mixture.

Refrigerate 2 to 3 hours or overnight. Bring to room temperature before cutting into bars.

Note: Like any no-bake cookie, the final texture of these really depends on how long you boil the sugar mixture. If it doesn't boil long enough, the cookie/bars mixture will be too soft, if you boil too long, they could turn out dry and crumbly.

CHOCOLATE OATMEAL BARS

NO BAKE   **15 MINUTE**

Easy Sweets

Printed in Great Britain
by Amazon